Prefixes and Suffixes

Careless!

Careful!

Unsafe!

written by Ann Heinrichs

illustrated by Dan McGeehan and David Moore

The Child's World

Published by The Child's World®
1980 Lookout Drive • Mankato, MN 56003-1705
800-599-READ • www.childsworld.com

ACKNOWLEDGMENTS
The Child's World®: Mary Berendes, Publishing Director
The Design Lab: Design and page production
Red Line Editorial: Editorial direction

LIBRARY OF CONGRESS CATALOGING-IN-PUBLICATION DATA
Heinrichs, Ann.
  Prefixes and suffixes / by Ann Heinrichs ; Illustrated by Dan McGeehan and David Moore.
      p. cm.
  Includes bibliographical references and index.
  ISBN 978-1-60253-430-8 (library bound : alk. paper)
  1. English language—Suffixes and prefixes—Juvenile literature.
  2. Language arts (Primary) I. McGeehan, Dan, ill. II. Moore, David, ill. III. Title.
  PE1175.H463 2010
  428.1—dc22   2010012343

Printed in the United States of America in Mankato, Minnesota.
July 2010
F11538

ABOUT THE AUTHOR

Ann Heinrichs was lucky. Every year from grade three through grade eight, she had a big, fat grammar textbook and a grammar workbook. She feels that this prepared her for life. She is now the author of more than 100 books for children and young adults. She has also enjoyed successful careers as a children's book editor and an advertising copywriter. Ann grew up in Fort Smith, Arkansas, and lives in Chicago, Illinois.

ABOUT THE ILLUSTRATORS

Dan McGeehan spent his younger years as an actor, author, playwright, cartoonist, editor, and even as a casket maker. Now he spends his days drawing little monsters!

David Moore is an illustration instructor at a university who loves painting and flying airplanes. Watching his youngest daughter draw inspires David to illustrate children's books.

Joyful!

TABLE OF CONTENTS

The Root of the Word

When I tie my shoes, I usually have to retie them. Please don't untie them.

What do tie, retie, and untie have in common? They all include the word tie. Tie is a **root word**. Root words are simple words. They are the base of more complicated words. What are the root words in these examples?

Please rewrite your story.

Watch out! The bridge is unsafe.

The root words are write and safe.

Adding Letters, Adding Meaning

How are retie and untie different?

Retie is re + tie.

Untie is un + tie.

Re and un are both **prefixes**. They come before root words.

Adding a prefix changes the meaning of a root word. When you retie your shoes, you're starting over. When you untie your shoes, you're taking out the knots.

More Prefixes

Yikes! The toilet is overflowing.

This hamburger is still pink. It's undercooked.

Over and under are two other prefixes. Over can mean too much. Under can mean not enough.

They can also mean just what they say—over (above) and under (below).

There's a flock of pigeons overhead.
The squirrel buried its acorns underground.

My dinner is overdone!

9

Prefix Numbers

Some prefixes show how many or how much.

A bicycle has two wheels.

A tricycle has three wheels.

A semicircle is a half circle.

A multicolored coat has many colors.

Prefix	Meaning
bi	two
tri	three
semi	half or partly
multi	many

Many More Prefixes

There are prefixes everywhere! Some common prefixes are de, dis, non, pre, and post.

The window is frosted. We need to defrost it if we want to see out.

I think you're wrong. I completely disagree with you.

Dad fried the eggs in a nonstick pan.

I bought pizza that is ready to eat. It is prebaked.

What do you call a party that happens after a football game? A postgame party.

Adding Letters at the End

The fearless monkey climbed the tree.
The fearful lion ran away.

How are fearless and fearful different? Ful and less are **suffixes**. They come after root words. Adding a suffix changes the meaning of the root word. Ful means with or full of something. Less means without or lacking something.

Fearless is fear + less.

Fearful is fear + ful.

Teachers and Dancers

One important suffix is er.

A teacher is someone who teaches.

A baker is someone who bakes.

A dancer is someone who dances.

Er goes with **verbs**, or action words. It helps show the person who does the action.

Verb	Person
teach	teacher
bake	baker
dance	dancer

17

Y and LY

Two common suffixes are y and ly. Y creates words that describe things.

Stop tracking mud into the house.
Get those muddy boots out of here!

Want to have fun? Watch a chimpanzee do funny tricks.

Ly creates words that describe how things happen.

I am quick.
I ran the race quickly.

The monsters are nice.
They behave nicely.

More Suffixes

There are many more suffixes. Some common ones are ous, ish, tion, ness, able, and ment.

I have fame. Everyone knows my name. I am famous.

I create drawings. My art is my creation.

The glass vase could break. It is breakable.

I am a fool. I do things that are foolish.

We are sad and blue. We feel sadness.

I watch the waves move. The movement makes me calm.

Big Words, No Problem!

Now that you know prefixes and suffixes, you can put together many big words.

prefix		root		suffix			big word
un	+	happy	+	ness		=	unhappiness
un	+	luck	+	y		=	unlucky
		joy	+	ful	+ ness	=	joyfulness
		cheer	+	ful	+ ly	=	cheerfully

I'll dance cheerfully!

How to Learn More

AT THE LIBRARY

Cerf, Chris. *Un People vs. Re People*. London: Golden Books, 2000.

McClarnon, Marciann. *Painless Junior Grammar*. Hauppauge, NY: Barron's Educational Series, 2007.

Ruscoe, Michael. *Pit Stop Prefixes*. Pleasantville, NY: Gareth Stevens, 2009.

Ruscoe, Michael. *Soccer Goal Suffixes*. Pleasantville, NY: Gareth Stevens, 2009.

Schoolhouse Rock: Grammar Classroom Edition. Dir. Tom Warburton. Interactive DVD. Walt Disney, 2007.

ON THE WEB

Visit our home page for lots of links about grammar: *childsworld.com/links*

NOTE TO PARENTS, TEACHERS AND LIBRARIANS: We routinely check our Web links to make sure they're safe, active sites—so encourage your readers to check them out!

Glossary

prefixes (PREE-fiks-iz): Letters that come at the beginning of words that change the meanings of those words. In *untie*, *un* is the prefix.

root word (ROOT WURD): A simple word that is the base of more complicated words. In *untie*, *tie* is the root word.

suffixes (SUHF-iks-is): Letters that come at the end of words that change the meaning of those words. In *cheerful*, *ful* is the suffix.

verbs (VURBS): Action words that describe things to do or ways to be. *Run* and *help* are both verbs.

(24)

Index